water on the moon

Mike Riddle

water on the moon

Acknowledgements

The following poems have been previously published:
'water on the moon', 'words' and 'what is left': *A Poetic Road Map:*
Wattletales: online
'approaching dusk': *tamba*: Autumn/Winter 2021, *Words to Share*
'pianissimo' and 'intoxication': *one talk*
'dismantled' and 'hissing': *Change Media_this breath is not mine to keep*
'gallery launch' and 'the blind mole and the cancer patient':
Ochre Ten, an anthology
'turning circles': published as 'Old Rogues' in *Platinum Poems*
'not my usual GP': *Three-cornered Hat*
'whale watching', 'life as it is' and 'love as it is': *Fleurieu Flow*

Much of *water on the moon* has been shared at Friendly Street Poetry
on the Fleurieu, Goolwa, and at Ochre Coast Poets, Seaford

Dedication

To the poets of the Fleurieu whose generosity, wisdom and artistry
has enriched my life in poetry and to those who have been of special
significance as the journey progressed, in chronological order of
meeting, Ruth Dennis, Jude Aquilina (patient and exquisite
mentor), Nigel Ford, Veronica and David Cookson, Geoff Aitken
and, before all, Marie.

Thank you to Stephen and Brenda at Ginninderra Press
for your generous understanding and support.

water on the moon
ISBN 978 1 76109 480 6
Copyright © text Mike Riddle 2023
Cover image: Pramod Tiwari from Unsplash

First published 2023 by
GINNINDERRA PRESS
PO Box 3461 Port Adelaide 5015
www.ginninderrapress.com.au

Contents

water on the moon	9
skipping	10
night glimpses	11
middle peninsula recall	12
indiscretions	13
awaiting the remarkable	14
approaching dusk	15
contentment	16
blink of an eye	17
ripe	18
strange ship	19
pianissimo	20
intoxication	21
a blessing of silt	22
tempus fugit	23
in practice	24
informed?	25
microcosms	26
beyond	28
pockmarks	29
dismantled	30
critical mass	33
screen addiction	34
cocooned	35
in the American summer of '69	36
down Conflict Street	37
Judas boxes	38
hissing	39
gallery launch	40
to the sensitive	41

turning circles	42
lifting edges	44
not my usual GP	45
walking Lake Gairdner	46
the blind mole and the cancer patient	48
they said – i said	49
changing thought	50
it wasn't me	51
should you adorn the wall	52
arrival	53
new year's bridge incident	54
lolly shop	57
whale watching	58
treasure chest	60
enveloped	61
the cipher's lament	62
the cipher's concession	63
still life with zombie	64
quoting Nabokov	65
Goolwa wharf precinct – winter	66
if publication is intended	67
ambiguous	68
attuned to aphids	69
life as it is	70
love as it is	72
from my window	73
in truth	74
draft horses	75
words	76
nine ways to kill time	77
what is left	78

finding the answers
it's a human obsession
but you might as well talk
to the stones and the trees and the sea

– Marillion

water on the moon

in October 2020 two papers published in *Nature Astronomy*
revealed there is water on the moon

casual voices in the ear
the theories of Hawking

brisk wind on the face
fat toads buried in the desert

>   the intuitive
>   and the counterintuitive

ice melting on the tongue
water on the moon

>   and in the hope of ages
>   the sharpened thorn
>   of enlightenment

skipping

for my mother 1923–2005

bones
brittle as magnesium strips
waiting to be lit
flesh
of softened pinks and purples
thin as bougainvillea petals
memory
of any memory
non-existent

yet when i read to you again
of Christopher Robin
going *hoppity hoppity hop*
the angel you became
left skipping

night glimpses

at pillow's touch
set the internal camera
to snare the ephemeral
that instant in dream
when loved ones lost
appear
resurrected
in purity of vision

middle peninsula recall

born Yorketown 1955

bitumen roads crusted grey
and brittle
bordered by wriggling lines
of dry-stone walls
shattered windmills that once pumped
for drought despairing farmers
salt lakes too shallow
to drown their thoughts
smoke rising in lines
from burn-offs

cliff edges not to be walked on
for fear of collapse
gulf waters shallow blue
and somnolent
oystercatchers imitating crows
at a distance
cormorants and fish
seagulls and chips

so rare the return
to my birthing place

i shed my snakeskins
long ago

indiscretions

in the town ringed by salt lake and barley bag
indiscretions sat on front-room window ledges
like collectible china ornaments
shivered at the milkman's clink of billycan
rattled to wind-carried street whispers
and front-bar sniggers before the six o'clock call

yet with night's arrival
they steadfastly remained
…and grew heavy
obscured by curtains

awaiting the remarkable

harvest taken
within the summer stubble
lies a manifestation of life
miniature magical six-legged

each stalk
gifts a shimmering golden shelter
where busying insects hide
and silently thrive

habitual observer
with sun's slow surrender
i await the remarkable
the cautious disclosure
of the coexisting Gulliver
amongst the minutiae of Lilliput

above the stubble shelf
rise the inverted Vs of roo ears

approaching dusk

the stained-glass river
is shattered
by the darter's knifing beak

blank canvas footpaths
are daubed
by streetlights' yellow gouache

night birds echo acoustic musicians
as whitewashing mist
smothers dulled day in harmony

contentment

the wind
that whips the river
to slap the wharf
wakens the mind
to the bite of spray
and to the give
of wood
beneath springing feet

blink of an eye

beach-walking in sunshine
by the shallows of despair
clinging to the hope
that within an eye's blink
the crow's shadow
can be cast
from the carrion mind

ripe

the lemon bergamot pear
still life in moon-crater fruit bowl

hides camouflaged among season's citrus
mandarins and namesake lemons

lacks the gleaming intensity of colour
the dimples of zest

but if raised and lightly finger-pressed
will announce its readiness

it's not the release of intoxicating fragrance
when the fruit knife cuts
nor the titillating taste
of pallid flesh

it's the magic of moment that matters
for this fruit has been treated
as nature deserves
and picked when ripe

strange ship

a no dog day –
on a detritus-strewn beach
wayward seagrass balls
crab carapaces and empty pipis
wave cast into sand's maw

an unhurried gull day –
eyes untroubled by glare or breeze
wander until arrested
by a bouquet-shaped sponge
sea bestowed at high tide

a stop to stoop day –
and closer examination reveals
an attachment of finest flowers
tousled filigree
and comely petite fans

an amend thoughts day –
for this is no flimsy garland
more a glorious
and strange ship
decaying
hull rust-red over buff
stricken sails crusted salt white
anchorage severed
and marooned
at the command
of the imperious ocean

this is a stamped in memory day –

pianissimo

in this absence
of tree
of shrub
in this hazardous heat
even the sounds
of a sympathetic piano
would be anomalous
to the pianissimo
of the desert symphony
of lizard eyes blinking
scorpion tails rising
hopping mice fidgeting
wind through hawk hover

observe
the orchestration of near silence

intoxication

with warmth of day
dying
the light brews
intricate ice blues
and periwinkles
toss and ferment
conditioning into
indigo clouds
full-bodied
primed to tempt the tongues
of West Coast grain growers
thirsty
for intoxicating rain

a blessing of silt

the derivation of humour is from Latin for liquid; a liquid it could
be said to have been distilled from the four ancient humours,
yellow bile, black bile, blood and phlegm

in this world of self-obsession
a drought of contentment
has sucked dry
merry humour
the liquid of laughter
from rebirth's river

let us awake
rebel
induce a maelstrom of mirth
pull asunder self-importance
drench catchments
until revelry floods
into each tributary's source
and as sprays of smiles
become a mighty stream
all can see
and become part of
a blessing of silt

tempus fugit

they swift step
those ticks of time
when choices
must be made
and fortune or failure
hang on a moment
leading to visions
of diamond or coal
amidst the sands
of the spinning hourglass

in practice

a moment's panic
a minute's elation
an hour's mischief
a day's accumulation
adhered to a dangling Möbius strip
spins in the blotting of clarity
and the blurring of before

it is thus we forget
it is thus we are forgotten

informed?

not always lucid
directions from a bus stop
not always factual
opinions in a front bar
not always relevant
books on a library shelf

not always considered
comments from the parochial
not always admissible
beliefs of the righteous
not always verified
claims by the political

microcosms

observations of birdlife; reflections on humanity

1.

swift flight of swallows
erratic and unpredictable
twitching tumbling
inherent from nest-leaving
designed perhaps
to elude hawks and falcons –
more an expression of elation

children squealing in a playground

2.

male masked lapwing
yellow-bespectacled
white-shirted
brown-suited
flies glides
direct and purposeful
to land in the centre of his grassy universe

an executive with no need for a briefcase

3.

white-capped galahs grey and pink
numbers ever changing
grass and seed scoffing
heads bobbing
mouths clacking
open and shut
in response to need or want

vegans chatting in a trendy café

4.

dishevelled black crow
plummets to earth
stands in feigned defiance
pounced on regardless
by black and white gangsters
pointed beaks taunting – jabbing
another joins the spree

local thugs know their victim

beyond

in times of fear or impending pain
thoughts fold and fold again
into the unproductive origami
of personal Hiroshimas
ignorant that beyond the horizon
on tranquil wings
approach flights
of resolute paper cranes

pockmarks

wrapped in thought
mired in memory
chronicling folly
slow dancing with regret
watching swallows swoop
spending days
spending days
spending days
awaiting the epiphany
the longed-for celebration
the mind's eradication
of past pockmarks
freeing the mouse
from its trap

dismantled

on nights of ample wind
through the open window
i can hear the waves
throbbing

borders
restrictions
cancellations
all gone viral

and in isolation
inspiration
diminished by demands
disappears
leaving this dreamer
floundering in a world
dis   man
        t   led

and yet
at times
i still hear the waves

these days I seem to think a lot
about the things that I forgot to do…
and all the times I had the chance to

– Jackson Browne

critical mass

in 1802 Wordsworth wrote of golden daffodils

over seventy-five years ago
the scientists ran the figures
knew the critical mass
of fissile material required
to achieve a self-sustaining
chain reaction
and to add mushroom
to the lexicon of clouds

between then and now
nestled in yet another cloud
definite article attached
the internet
has ushered in a new critical mass
requiring neither scientists nor figures
merely access
to execute
its omnipresence
its omnipotence
its…rightness

today
as yesterday
while the critical mass
mined and coal-fired the silence
i wandered lonely in the cloud
immersed in the sickly yellow
of a jaundiced social media

screen addiction

thinking compartmentalised
day's warped vision attained
through obedient application
to windows of dross and deceit
that fracture mental health
into prison block partitions

when the cage rattles
resist the addiction
evade the subtle snare of screen
break open the cell door
and succumb to the sunset

cocooned

she is bound in a cocoon of her own spinning
wrapped by thread of storyline
from radio and tablet
desperate tv news

windows misted
endlessly dressing-gowned
and coffee-cupped
gifted with the archaeologist's acumen
for unearthing secrets
fearless she ferrets
seeks world's worst
captures catastrophe
in word and image

lives life no longer suffering
a crisis of confidence
but determinedly nurturing
a confidence in crises

in the American summer of '69

(i was fourteen)

watching
Ken Burns's 2017 epic
The Vietnam War
and reflecting upon
Ho Chi Minh and LBJ
My Lai and Kent State
and Richard Tipping's *Soft Riots/TV News*
i've recognised that
over the crisp disintegration of years
having not stolen
the creative power of fire
to feed humankind's belly or brain
i am no Prometheus
but lacking in cunning and hubris
nurtured on my mother's fear
of tumbling dominoes
as a pale and faulty Sisyphus
i have rolled my guilt-ridden
adolescent-grown indecision
of what to do
what to believe
as rounded stone
partially up hill
only to step aside and let it fall again
…and again

in December of '72
i was six months from turning eighteen
and i thank Gough my marble never dropped

down Conflict Street

there is a consoling beauty
in the astute sidestep
from established path
that briefly and delicately
tramples neither weed nor bloom
but allows continuing vision

yet should fixed way and byway
become boulder strewn
and raindrop fall
fail to weather
the time may come
not for the cleaving of stone
but for the climbing above

Judas boxes

Bolsonaro's Brazil, 2020

in the funeral parlours
the cardboard boxes
are SOLD OUT

        now they're arrayed
        in barren fields
        side by side

occupants deceased and unattended
sold out for thirty pieces of silver
to support a fracturing economy

in crowded underprepared hospitals
exhausted health care workers
envisage the future and realise
a Judas box is theirs
for the taking

once the new stock arrives

hissing

a world
assumed secure
is hissing
seething
a symphony of sibilants

societies subside
saturated with suffering
share markets slump
stagger to a standstill
soldiers stand
saluting the sarcophagus of sanity

again the serpent has escaped the garden

gallery launch

i spy with my little eye

faces of scalded milk
and beach-lingered leather
skin flaps and seborrheic warts
scrutiny-seeking spectacles
and discreet earpieces
hair in thinning silver rivulets
or magicked memories of colour

some of the gathered
earrings jangling
are clothed in mottled parrot
and gaudy paraphernalia
to honour the artist

leaning against the railings
a hierarchy of hip replacement

yet there too
is a singular face
taut of skin
androgynous
beauty
distant and unresponsive

to the artistic ratification of ageing

to the sensitive

as the petals fall
one
by one
by one
until
there is no more
than a barren heart
remember
this is where the bee supped
to sweeten other lives

turning circles

for Wal and Amy

their eyes waltz
reflecting affection for that lost identity
and an allure towards that misplaced time
when social pressures were structured
soldiering and sacrifice built character
surviving depressions fostered spirit
and making do
did

their voices waltz
echoing the attraction of a Saturday night out
and the assurance of institute concerts
when blind men played talking violins
charity and occasion linked community
infants played angels with halos of tinsel
and the flicks
flickered

their bodies no longer waltz
the ripples on the tired flesh
of shoulders neck and brow
present too great a burden
for those limbs which
long to be turning circles
whirling
twirling

they do not waltz
but with roguish stares
and teasing words
lift themselves
and beckon
their memories
to play louder
louder

and they dance
without leaving their chairs

lifting edges

akin to aged skin

the corners of the paper
covering the complicated cardboard
begin to curl

        the effect of horse-hoof glue
        is waning

yellowing and crisp
wavering in their intent
the edges are lifting

        the façade of pleasantries past
        is peeling

this thin sheet
is forfeiting its purpose
preparing to falter

        and as with all before
        prodigious time threatens

not my usual GP

it was a momentary decision
not to read my medical history carefully
perhaps he was running late
or incompetent
or tired
or incompetent
or otherwise preoccupied
or incompetent
but for me his misdiagnosis was the catalyst
that started this chain of events
that brings each day
torment and ecstasy

and now after my catharsis
my reaching the point of no return
on an unchosen road less travelled
i write
because of passion
i write
because of love
i write
because of hope

and with hope
there is some chance of good

and so
his momentary decision
has led to a chance of good

or so i tell myself

walking Lake Gairdner
anaesthesia

heat heavy
ironed flat and desolate
the lake stretches beyond
the gathering point

                          prior to surgery
                          form-filling
                          light banter
                          observations taken

sun-glinted
a bracelet of foothills
the subtle salt layer
invites the traveller

                          change room
                          gown and hat
                          disposable shoes
                          dignity dismissed

wire missing
sinking with distance
wood-rotten fenceposts
offer no guidelines

                          waiting room
                          warm blanket
                          taciturn strangers
                          past experience dilutes fear

evenly spaced
gently salt-cracking
stamp of three-toed emu
prints small warnings

                              operating theatre
                              metallic table
                              methodical staff
                              acceptance of process

walking now
with each judicious step
the brittle crust snaps
and the thick ooze rises

                              the jaunt into the murk
                              begins with a slight scratch
                              on the barren surface
                              of the skin

the blind mole and the cancer patient

notoryctes typhlops: the southern marsupial mole

burrows where it
                cannot see

suffers what it
                cannot predict

falls prey to creatures it
                cannot deny

knows no fear

while in our world
inside the sparkling Tennyson Centre
to those who fear everything
come monthly encounters
with the softly padded chairs
of chemotherapy infusion
battleground with what
                cannot be seen
                        predicted
                              denied

and though many may fall
those who survive
become as blind moles
afraid of nothing
and climb
to nibble the tips at the top of eucalypts

they said – i said

they said
the tattoo artist's needles
make statements
ink beliefs desires motifs

i said
tattoos are colourful deceptions
until present fades to future
inspiration falls to melancholy

they said
go on…
get yourself a tatt

i said
i already have three
i got mine in the cancer ward

changing thought

for Jen and Carl

creative thinkers
scintillate as flakes
of colloidal silver
suspended
distinct
in a clever solution
of their own choosing

changing another's thought
can be as difficult
as pulling a single starling
from a swirling murmuration
can be as distant
as touching the nearest star
pitched against the night's blackness

yet still they try

it wasn't me

in memory of those wronged

it wasn't me
who made you seek a special space
it wasn't me
who made you loop the rope over the beam
it wasn't me
who made you tie the knot
it wasn't me
who made you place your head in the noose
it wasn't me
who kicked away the chair
it wasn't me
who accepted death without struggling
it was you

i just called you a slut
a skanky slut
not that any of the boys would have anything to do with you
not that i ever had anything to do with you
i never knew you
it's just that you were on the list
the list
i need to return to
it's more fun than any other game
i've ever played online
goodbye slut

time to play again

hello you
you slut…

should you adorn the wall

should you adorn the wall
prop as paper doll against it
head dangling
teeth chipped
motionless
beside the sticky slip
of blood
it is because

your strength is short of my weakness
your devotion is short of my indifference
your patience is short of my impatience
your restraint short of my lack of control

it is for you
to beg forgiveness

>   should you adorn the wall
>   why should i be punished?

approximately ninety-five per cent of Australian victims of domestic violence are female

arrival

drawn to the rabbit hole
as Alice
you espied an invitation
a welcoming
and after swallowing
a bottle of pills
labelled *Eat Me*
stepped into the darkness
fell
with the anticipation
of a soft landing
or at least the divesting
of melancholy

but to satisfy
the curious and the curiouser
you must be asked
was contentment found
upon arrival?

and what happened
when the Cheshire Cat stopped grinning?

new year's bridge incident

a jump into the unknown

post-midnight
there is an incident on the bridge
snatches of red/blue/red/blue
oppose the ash-greyed sky

cars stuffed with the homeward bound
wriggle as processionary caterpillars
before succumbing to paralysis

opened doors and lowered windows
offer possible theories
but the truth is a firework unexploded

and will I wait forever beside the silent mirror
and fish for bitter minnows amongst the weeds
and slimy water

– Genesis

lolly shop

a woman enters a lolly shop and says
i'll have a bag of mixed maxims…please

receives

inspiration is the dragon
that enflames the leaden spirit

trust is the aspirin
against the migraine of despair

art is the decoration
on the walls of the soul

envy is the conjoined twins
of love and betrayal

knowledge is the sledgehammer
against the high-rise of ignorance

smiling

she snatches the bag
and leaves without paying

whale watching

rough-edged scalpel
slices the sheet of ocean
to reveal a sliver of whale
thin pencil line – 3B dark
and nothing more

                i watch inspired
                my desire to write
                monstrous

drawn to its rise
my astute eyes fix
imagine the behemoth
beneath the rippling surface
bulbous and magical

                thoughts bob and swirl
                words submerged
                primed to breach

binoculars in hand
clarity increases
but this artwork
refuses to exhibit its greater self
declare its exquisite lumpy beauty

obsessed
i want my whale
to launch itself
beyond the scalpel cut
to project
beyond the stars
to display
every molecule
of its spectacular being

        but as black pen daubs paper
        i fear the slip of real whale
        will sink through the ocean's slit
        and disappear
        into the deepest chill
        of memory

treasure chest

holding her book in my hand
i drift and i am drifting
to jagged peninsulas of words
islands of insight
with no hint of piracy
exposed for all to see
her treasure chest

her poems

having read once
i cannot again turn the page
bested as i am by

her poems

the book in my hand exudes
the smell of sex
of sunshine
of carrots turnips parsnips and barley
and this warming broth
speed dials why we are here
why we write
she – in her fecundity
i – in my void

the poems

enveloped

upon arrival
Ruth's letters
hand-written
hook and link
not with clanking chains
of joyless emails
and semblance of attachment
but with multihued ribbon
of immeasurable length
refusing to fray
threading separation
with rippling veins of life

the cipher's lament

definition of cipher: zero; person of no influence

wishing
wanting
yearning
to be more
the cipher
wallowing
in a black hole
awaits his big bang
or at least
a one-hit wonder…

…squeals with delight
in the knowledge
of his ability to compute
that a trillion times zero
is…

the cipher's concession

definition of cipher: zero; person of no influence

Turing unlocked the Enigma machine
the enigma that was Joyce unloosed Ulysses
Ulysses unravelled language
Lawrence's language unbuttoned Lady Chatterley
Lady Chatterley undid morality
morality unfastened…

…and on and on
the cherished marks of history and literature
manacled to the cipher's concession
that contrary to his status
some are greater than zero

still life with zombie

sunlight parachutes through glass
sprinkles on the stained leather recliner
and shivers
on touching the stillness
of the decaying form
bloated
as a roadkill bullock
grotesque in its quietude
and the covering of gauzy wings
plucked from houseflies

the lace-clothed side table
unevenly weighted
hosts a book
mote smothered
and a softened shortbread
while a pottery mug of unfinished coffee
grows a plethora of blue fibres
cornflowers in a circled garden

to one side
the corpse's wife
the zombie
stands snatching flies from mid-air
detaching wings
awaiting her husband's transformation

quoting Nabokov

'the evolution of sense is, in a sense, the evolution of nonsense' –
Nabokov

so common in its uncommonness
the senselessness of sense
that reason without reasoning
demands sharp recompense
thus magi without magic
with closed vision open wide
commanding backward forward steps
should agree to be denied
not realise their fantasies
in their halting ceaseless puffing
but absorb their own effusions
for they lead…
           to the lessened ends of nothing

Goolwa wharf precinct – winter

Ngarrindjeri images
cut deep into fallen timbers
Signal Point breezeway
torments cheek and neck
letters writ large lacerate
the incongruous chalkboard

                links unclear

whiff of wharf surrenders
to sourness of spilt craft beer
Barrel Shed conversation forfeited
to the lapping of the black river
dark railway station shadows
fade into nothingness grey

                bonds tenuous

peer into the last light
and as rail tracks
parallel
stretch
until distance says
they touch

                the poem
                hunted for
                is snared

if publication is intended

as droplets spill
from tips of weighted leaves
to dry and disappear
without replenishing the earth
words of pale beauty
subtle and virtuous
slip between the imperatives
of self-satisfaction and commercialism
and surrendering aspiration
slide into sharp-edged envelopes
marked
return to sender

ambiguous

thoughts disparate
hang

cloud like midges
nourished by the politics
of approval and dissent
to distil or to die
in solitude

counsel
or lip service
demigods or nitpickers
poets critiquing

attuned to aphids

the published poet and reviewer
with words inextricably interdependent
as notes in a scale
harmonic –
        avoid any propensity to discord
boldly seeking symbiosis
as ants
attuned to aphids

life as it is

supermarket – the phone rings
fat fingers fumble
too slow to respond
call missed
so i ring

we are unavailable at the moment…if you wish to leave…
i do (wish to leave)
i press end

eggs – i want eggs
aisle 2 – there's a sign
but no sign of eggs

free range eggs are unavailable at the moment…
no eggs

take ticket at butchers
butcher has beef lamb pork chicken venison
schnitzels kebabs rissoles satays nuggets
mullet prawns abalone scallops
but no eggs

phone rings again
are you available at the moment to see your...
i don't pay much attention
it could be my GP
oncologist
endocrinologist
gastroenterologist
neurologist (eight jabs of Botox)
for a parotidectomy
colonoscopy
endoscopy
vocal cord medialisation
neuromodulation insertion
garrotting
strangling
drawing and quartering

no i'm not available
inside my addled mind
i'm writing a poem
and i'm available for nothing

life as it is

love as it is

lover please believe for it is true
when i say i *in brackets* (almost) love you

and that throughout my days
i will *in brackets* (almost) love you *in brackets* (always)

therefore countless times even when thoughts form anew
i will *in double brackets* ((almost always)) love you

from my window

clouds
windblown white camellias
petal a sky
fickle as a gigolo's promise

bees
pinstriped businessmen
penetrate correa bells
inviting as a hooker's smile

crested pigeons
coo and jockey for position
bob as lusty buoys
on a lawn green ocean

hopelessly longing for potency
or relevance
i close the curtains
and look in on myself

the percentage of damaged poets
increased again this quarter
the ABS announced today

in truth

a life spent
beguiled by promise
afflicted by doubt
and the restraints of reality
leading sensibly
inevitably
into being
wedged into inconsequence
part of the flock
indistinguishable
and indiscriminately screeching
as little corellas
on their summer sojourn

draft horses

in instants of creative stasis
pause to recall artists
the ilk
of Becket Namatjira Heysen
whose brief incandescence
gifted light
as Aurora Australis
shimmering above
we draft horses
of the darkly ploughed paddocks

Clarice Beckett 1887–1935
Albert Namatjira 1902–1959
Sir Hans Heysen 1887–1968

words

as darts at a board
tips forever gnashing at iron
and falling as lethal whispers
to the floor

nine ways to kill time

snuff out a candle clock
cover a sundial with a hangman's hood
push an hourglass under a butcher's truck
take a grandfather clock to the rifle range
smash a watch with a sledgehammer
incinerate a perpetual calendar
detonate an atomic clock
write a meaningless poem about killing time
read a meaningless poem about killing time

what is left

staring southward at low tide
sighting the contradiction
of pelagic corridors
the existence of pathways
through the incessant turmoil
of waves and fluid lives
confusion arrives
with a kiss of foam

what is left
but to write
within limitations